D1606923

FUSION

LIFE WORKS!

CAN'T DO IT ALL

HOW TO FIND BALANCE

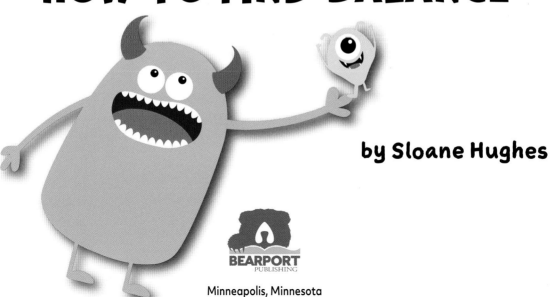

by Sloane Hughes

BEARPORT
PUBLISHING

Minneapolis, Minnesota

Credits: 4, © Vectorfair/Shutterstock; 5, © acidmit/Shutterstock, © bungacengkeh/Shutterstock, © RedlineVector/Shutterstock; 6, © White Space Illustrations/Shutterstock; 7, © VALUA VITALY/Shutterstock; 8, © wavebreakmedia/Shutterstock; 9, © Diwas Designs/Shutterstock, © Panda Vector/Shutterstock, © Moyo Studio/iStock, © Halfpoint/iStock; 11, © YummyBuum/Shutterstock, © Colorlife/Shutterstock; 12, © RealPeopleGroup/iStock, © Khosrork/iStock; 13, © Irina Belova/iStock; 15, © Roi and Roi/Shutterstock, © ansveta/Shutterstock; 17, © Sergey Novikov/Shutterstock; 20, © Yevheniia Rodina/Shutterstock; 21, © Riccardo Mayer/Shutterstock; 22, © Africa Studio/Shutterstock; 23, © Africa Studio/Shutterstock, © Hogan Imaging/Shutterstock.

Bearport Publishing Company Product Development Team
President: Jen Jenson; Director of Product Development: Spencer Brinker; Managing Editor: Allison Juda; Associate Editor: Naomi Reich; Senior Designer: Colin O'Dea; Associate Designer: Elena Klinkner; Associate Designer: Kayla Eggert; Product Development Specialist: Anita Stasson

Library of Congress Cataloging–in–Publication Data is available at www.loc.gov or upon request from the publisher.

ISBN: 979–8–88509–964–6 (hardcover)
ISBN: 979–8–88822–141–9 (paperback)
ISBN: 979–8–88822–284–3 (ebook)

For more information, write to Bearport Publishing, 5357 Penn Avenue South, Minneapolis, MN 55419.

SO MUCH

There are so many fun things out there. We may want to do it all. But that can make us really busy really fast!

CONTENTS

When we take on too much, it doesn't feel good. So, we have to be smart as we pick things to do.

YOU DECIDE

Balance is about making sure our lives have the right amounts of different things. When we have good balance, we feel better!

Sometimes, we have to make choices about what we do in order to keep good balance. It might mean saying no to some things. This can make us feel like we are missing out. But it is better to do fewer things well than to do too much.

Think about the last time you had to choose between two things. How did you pick?

YOUR PRIORITIES

How can we choose the right things to do? To start, we think about our **priorities**, or what's important to us. We can put those things first.

Doing well in school might be a priority.

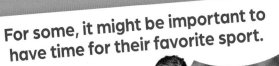
For some, it might be important to have time for their favorite sport.

Staying healthy should be a priority. We need to eat well and get good sleep.

My priority is to cook the perfect slug!

9

SEEING IS BELIEVING

Keeping your priorities in sight can remind you what is most important.

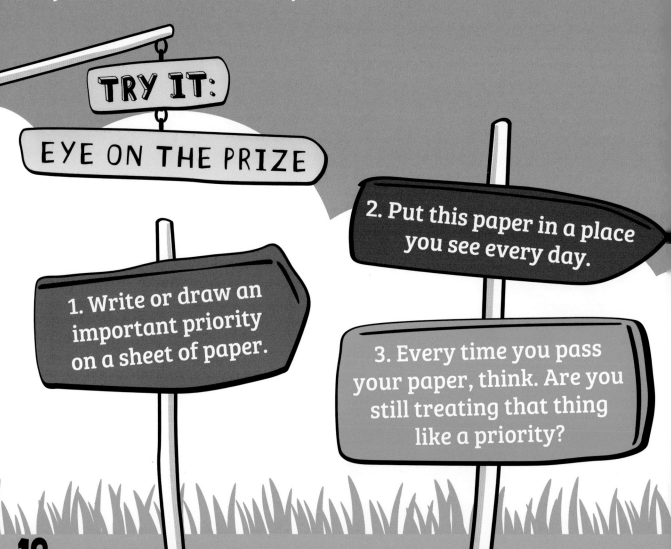

TRY IT:

EYE ON THE PRIZE

1. Write or draw an important priority on a sheet of paper.

2. Put this paper in a place you see every day.

3. Every time you pass your paper, think. Are you still treating that thing like a priority?

11

GETTING STARTED

We can do a lot of things and still keep balance when we are smart about how we use our time.

Making a plan before we get started helps us know what to **expect**.

Finishing the most important tasks first means following our priorities.

Setting time **limits** can help us **focus**.

TAKING TIME

Keep track of your time to help you focus on getting a task done.

TRY IT:

FAST FOCUS

1. Pick something you need to do that can be finished quickly.

2. Set a timer for 5 minutes.

3. Focus on only that thing for the whole time.

4. When the timer goes off, check out how much you've done.

5. If you need more time, give yourself another 5 minutes.

15

HERE AND HAPPY

Getting our priorities done makes us feel great! But we need to balance priorities with doing things we love just because.

That can mean taking a break from studying to make time for our family and friends. Keeping things that make us happy in our **schedules** should also be a priority.

PLAN IT

Put your happiness on the schedule!

TRY IT:

A HAPPY CALENDAR

2. Get a special calendar and some stickers.

3. Put a sticker on the calendar every day you do one of the activities.

1. Write or draw a list of small activities that make you happy.

4. How many stickers can you get?

19

CHANGES

Sometimes, staying balanced means making changes. Our lives are changing all the time. Our priorities should, too!

Some days, things become too much. Other times, we find we can do more. It's okay to **adjust** what we have planned.

Think of the last time a change helped you stay balanced. How did it make you feel?

BALANCE IS BEST

We can't do it all. But we can make choices that keep us happy and healthy. It's all about balance!

23

GLOSSARY

adjust to change something to make it better

expect to think about what would or could happen

focus to give your full attention to something

limits the points beyond which a person or thing cannot go

priorities things that are the most important

schedules plans for what to do when

INDEX